FROM THE ASHES

RHYMES ABOUT RISING

Tasia Gill

BookLeaf Publishing

India | USA | UK

Presentation by *BookLeaf Publishing*

Web: www.bookleafpub.com

E-mail: info@bookleafpub.com

ISBN: 9789358739039

First edition 2023

PREFACE

I became aware of my life cycles when I was a teenager. It seemed every two years I was experiencing a major shift that would reveal my naivety and required me to reimagine the way I saw the world. When I became an adult, the cycles remained two years long and the lessons would intensify the higher I vibed. What I learned from this is that when you search for your most authentic truth, the universe has a way of making things fall apart so that they fall into place. And it was the sages I met along my path that would share their wisdom- small words of encouragement or stories of their own evolution; that encouraged me to keep going, knowing that the divine ways of nature would always be with me in my favor. Rising to your highest truth takes time. You are an evolution within an ever-evolving dimension and to heal yourself is to heal the world. Keep going.

DEDICATION

To those on their path- Remain vigilant in your desire to rise and ever willing to let go of notions that no longer serve you.

1. A TALK WITH OUR REFLECTION

I don't remember when it happened.

I don't remember when you abandoned the blissful ignorance to darkness and chose to live

in fear.

I don't remember why.

I don't remember when you began to think you might not perform being yourself as well as you hoped.

I don't remember when you started guarding your heart in fear of bleeding to death.

I don't remember when you started to reject love because it never came without pain.

I don't remember when you started running.

Yes, running from success because your wounds tell you you'll lose what you love.

I don't remember what silenced your loud heart and snuffed out your highest light.

What is it? What is it that made you think you had to live small so as not to rise and soar out of fear you'll crash and burn.

No more, dearest you.

Today is a new day.

Today you ignite anew- the flame within.

2. THE TRUTH BEHIND ME

Lay down your burdens and unpack your wounds.

Show me the darkest corner of your ruins.

Reveal the last breath of your whimsical mind.

How I would give anything to bring you back in time.

Take me to the place where your mouth finds your words.

Show me the fork in your heart where the road starts to curve.

Tell me what your fears eat and who lives in your past.

Walk me along the shore of your pain's aftermath.

Show me the place where your shackled trust fights

Take me to the place where your tears have gone dry.

Unpack your wounds and show me everything

Leave it all right here, the pain and the suffering.

Now look at yourself, your beautiful reflection!

Free from the ash and painful recollection.

Now live on in love, the past will set with the sun.

For you are purely love and forever your only one.

3. TRIGGERS AND TRAUMA

Ripples of fear touching every thought.

Warnings of flames that never rage hot.

Memories distorted with opaque recollection.

Heaven turned to hell with a semblance of introspection.

Easy turned hard.

Hot turned cold.

Lies in the moment from erroneous stories told.

Innocence is guilt.

Healing is pain.

Growing out of it hurts 'cause you'll never be the same.

4. IMPOSTER SYNDROME

Mosaics with soft edges, I no longer bleed.

A mirror voids a reflection and a breath can now breathe.

Rare diamonds made of dust.

Gentle visions of blue trust.

Eyes veiled with truth.

Unbridled will to move.

5. RAISE YOUR VIBRATION

In a pool of lukewarm, I start to feel cold as the pages of mendacities crumble and fold.

Floating low, overgrown in flesh and robe

Awaiting transition from this dimension in strobe.

To rise, I long; To emerge, I must

Confidence in my authenticity; abound to combust.

No more to gain in this space; higher I must strive

Vibration rise.

Abundantly thrive.

On to live my highest truth, fully alive.

6. BEYOND THIS MOMENT

I stand paralyzed at the edge of my ending

Afraid to incinerate the past for a new beginning.

I long to see with brand new eyes, no lies

A time where trauma doesn't speak

And my wings, with wind beneath them fly.

I plunge, wrapped in hope into the flame and burn it all down.

For the only way to rise is through the ashes while they're still hot on the ground.

7. REJECTION WOUND

It's becoming too much to bare- this fear of being seen.

This chance that pain will be the only thing I'll ever be.

In the qualms of identity, I'm poised to see

The rambunctious way I can unapologetically be me.

8. RISE

The dire feat of fear stands riddled with possibility unearthed.

We hide from our potential to feel safe in the doubt they gave us at birth.

No longer can we stand to breathe the division and malice they've doomed us to reap.

The promise to rise is one we must intend to keep.

To rise against the past.

To rise against the lies.

To rise against the divide.

To rise up with valor and pride.

Keeping our faith strong in our stride.

No longer will we conform and abide

To live almost dead and not fully alive.

9. ABANDONMENT WOUND

Dear John,

I don't like the way things are going between you and I.

Being rejected by you is too painful to chance and I no longer feel alive.

I've started to shut down parts of me to avoid said rejection

So many parts of me keep dying, of myself I have no recollection.

Did you know I must muster up courage just to call you?

I must muster up the arms to bare a loss neither certain nor true.

It's the abandonment wound that breaks me to pieces unglued.

It's easier to end it before it begins, as I cannot fathom losing you.

So I think we should end it now and just simply be friends.

It's better this way- to bring the inevitable to a timely end.

-Jane

10. A FORMAL LETTER

It is with a stark assurance that I must note

"Good" intentions seldom linger through valleys of the invoked

It is with immense regret, I must inform you

People shift like the seasons and tend to mold like conformed views.

It pains my heart, but I have to be frank

Hard lessons make you break and cut deep like a prison shank.

To the end of the edge of a never ending cycle

Of a bridled affair with love on a tightrope bound in a blindfold.

Though dimensions have blurred and the black hole is dark

Your temple burns a light that get's brighter with each fresh start.

So believe in that clock. Timing is always right.

It's never too late to leap into the bright.

11. BURN ME TO THE GROUND

Hate will be the death of me if I die in it's grip.

A breath of fresh love as a cure, get me an intravenous drip.

Forgiveness, not acceptance

Forgetting my own repentance.

A test of my courage

A courage to trust

Burn me to the ground

Await my rise from the dust.

12. A SIMPLE QUESTION

WoMan's most unanswered question- Why am I here?

We're born without the knowledge to be civilized

But we know how to crawl to our mother's breast to drink milk.

When does that force of nature abandon us?

13. ONE

Let's talk about the experience of the Earthling.

The journey of infinite energy.

The dimensions of that divine spark of light living a human life

And the moments of serendipity and synergy.

You'll find that when the connective source leads our human vessel

That harmonious results most certainly ensue.

Whatever we need, we will be drawn to it and it to us.

It is an effortless dance when our intuition leads.

That Is God.

We are all part of the same algorithm

That is Mother Nature.

The laws of our body are the laws of Planet Earth.

So Earthlings, remember, we are all intertwined.

One energy.

One source.

One vine.

14. A NOTE TO SELF

All I can control in life is my actions and reactions.

I can't undo anything, I can't prevent everything

And I cannot decide every fate.

I'm dealt the hand I'm dealt

And I use intelligence to move beyond moments of trial and error.

In my happiest days, darkness can loom

And in my darkest days, light can overcome.

So, may I gracefully release the cumbersome unknown

And embrace my individual strength.

So that as life continues to kick my ass and throw me in a bed of roses

I may stand firm in who I am.

15. RANDOM THOUGHT

A memory of the past can wreak havoc on a moment.

Cowardice, as a result is reborn each fateful morning.

With just a quick gust of fear

An enemy, armed with envy painstakingly appears.

Leave not yourself open to be taken down the path of confusion

Darkness often blinds us and out of nothing creates an illusion.

The firmest reality is hidden in your existence

And this, you will find with an open 6th and persistence.

Chakras must be balanced.

Energy must be neutral.

The elements of your dimensions?

Alignment is undoubtedly crucial.

16. WAKING UP

When I open my eyes, I open wide.

A dark and failed truth, I can no longer abide.

Fistfuls of rest and leaps of growth in stride.

Naked in truth, I will not hide.

Rising with the moon, I am the tide.

17. BE SEEN

So, whoever meets you- may they see exactly what you choose to be.

Remain nude in your truth as it will always be there for the world to see.

Let your skin transcend you so that you may live spiritually.

See others in their purest light and expand your highest vibrancy.

Surf the vibe of your tribe and sail the seas of potency.

Perfection in moderation- retreat in pools of purity.

Seek to mistake

Evolve and remake

Revel in your transparency.

18. INNER CHILD

I can smell the dirt beneath my fingernails.

I can feel minerals of earth on my feet.

I can taste the rain on my lips.

I can see the story of today on my knees.

The child at play, who plays hard.

She strays for the day but never goes far.

She adventures the backroads and is mindful of the time.

Unknowingly crossing bounds and innocently committing crimes.

Unafraid to spell her world into existence.

Creating unbridled and achieving with persistence.

Who told her she couldn't do this?

Who lied and laid the barrier around her space.

For she is now grown up and has left behind her world for a new place.

19. HURT PEOPLE HURT PEOPLE

I didn't mean to

And I know you didn't either

But hurt people hurt people.

I know your pain manifested a blade

And cut me deep.

I cut you, too and together we bleed.

This Capulet dance is toxic

I can no longer die for you.

For I am mine

And you are yours.

The Earth is green

The Water is blue.

20. HEALTHY LOVE

Let me tell you about healthy love.

Healthy love transcends your bleeding trauma

And reveals healing paths to your highest light.

Healthy love is few of words

And plentiful of action.

Healthy love admires your past

Celebrates your present

And holds hope for your future.

Healthy love sees you

And respects you from the start.

On the contrary

Healthy love has no beginning

For healthy love is a way of the heart.

21. REEMERGE

With the ashes still hot

After your proverbial demise

Save space for the courage

To raise fiercely

And continuously rise.

Never look back

Or be bogged by what purged.

For no part of you is broken

You are whole again

Reemerged.

22. CLASHING VIBES

From friction to fire

A spark ignites a flame

And dirt melts to mire

23. CHAKRA IMBALANCE

Harrowing hearts and brittle minds

Weak autonomy and lost paths

Withdrawn from the moon but open to the night.

Withering hope and faulty throats

Weak words and lost thoughts

Withdrawn from your power but open to fight.

Shattering sentiments and haughty portrayals

Weak sensations and lost battles

Withdrawn from yourself but open to the light.

24. THE WILLOW THAT SPOKE

A willow spoke to me today

She told me of her life

And of the things she'd seen.

The proposals and the mourning,

The deaths and the lynching.

She told me about the woman

Who spread her husband's ashes around her trunk.

And about the daughter of that woman

Who spread hers there, too.

She spoke about a traveler who'd slept under her branches

And read poetry at night.

She told me how the traveler prayed for better days.

The willow says she spoke to the traveler, as they'd asked her to show them the way.

The willow told the traveler their path was invaluable

That hard times are spiritual instruction from the Light.

She said the traveler grew peaceful

And continued to pray through the night.

The willow is wise

And she weeps for her earth-mate.

"Do they not know their strength?" She asks

"With roots deep, they can withstand the storm"

I told the willow the path of WoMan is complex

For we are victims of our culture

And our own species, we do not respect.

The willow understood and continued to weep.

25. MOUNTAIN TOP

Within each of us lies

An inkling to express our pain.

Take heart, for it is our voice

Rising to be heard.

With love, I beckon you

To use your voice

To cry out your triumph.

For pain has no place atop your mountain.

Nay, I say It belongs on the path you walked to summit.

Cry out your triumphs and heed the call to your purpose.

26. ALL THE NOTHING WAS PURGED

As every notion continued to burn

My spirit revealed·a new truth.

New hopes emerged

I burned to nothing

And all the nothing was purged.

27. PERFECTION WITHIN

A new path is a fresh start

And a healed heart hath no wrath.

For in light there is no darkness

And in God there is no sin.

So seek the wisdom of Nature

And find perfection within.

28. A FLAME IGNITED

I wrote a letter to myself

And I addressed it to the day.

I shared how the rhythm of

My vibration hummed a warning

That I shouldn't stay.

The letter, I flouted.

I went on against my verdict.

A betrayal for a flame ignited

And a truth for a lie incited.

29. REBIRTH

When you return,

Forget what died with you.

Move forward with

New eyes opened wide.

Fully alive

Time anew

Live in full bloom

Live full for you.

30. PRAYED FOR

She wished upon a star one night

For an Angel to appear.

Instead of one, she got two

But in one she saw no fear.

This Angel of light would warm her path

And brave her greatest fall.

She asked for one, but needed two

And the light? She named him Saul.

9 789358 739039